Soul Retreats™

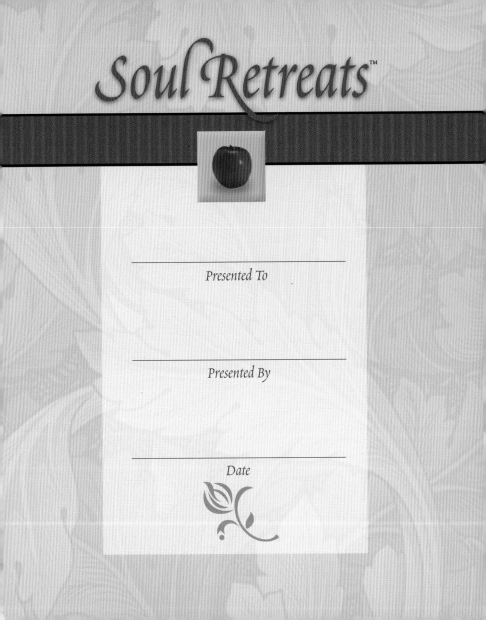

_____

Presented To

_____

Presented By

_____

Date

Soul Retreats™ for Teachers
ISBN 0-310-98901-9

Copyright 2002 by GRQ Ink, Inc.
1948 Green Hills Boulevard
Franklin, Tennessee 37067

"Soul Retreats" is a trademark owned by GRQ, Inc.

Published by Inspirio™, The gift group of Zondervan
5300 Patterson Avenue, SE
Grand Rapids, Michigan 49530

Requests for information should be addressed to:
Inspirio™, The gift group of Zondervan
Grand Rapids, Michigan 49530

http://www.inspiriogifts.com

Editor and Compiler: Lila Empson
Associate Editor: Janice Jacobson
Project Manager: Tom Dean
Manuscript written and prepared by Melinda Mahand
Design: Whisner Design Group

Soul Retreats™
for Teachers

inspirio™

Contents

Introduction

As a teacher, you spend the vast majority of your time giving of yourself to others. Students, parents, coworkers, and your own friends and family members all come to you for guidance and direction. But do you crave a few moments of private introspection, a time when you can receive encouragement and assurance from the Lord? If so, turn to the fifteen-minute meditations of *Soul Retreats*™ *for Teachers*. The uplifting insights and affirmations within these pages will allow you a few precious moments to suspend the many demands of your day and enjoy a time of reflection with the Lord.

You may browse through the meditation titles and choose each day the selection that addresses your present need, or you may prefer to simply read the meditations in the order they are printed. Either way, you will discover strength and understanding spoken directly to the heart of a teacher and designed to refresh and renew your soul.

His Voice

How, Lord, do I listen?
For your voice speaks in ocean waves as they crash to the shore.
How, Lord, do I listen?
For your voice speaks in thunder blasts as heavy rain showers pour.

Is there a Word for me that I can hear within the quiet of my soul?
Is there a Word for me that once again will heal and make me whole?

Teach me, Lord, to listen.
For I am waiting eagerly; I long to hear your voice.
Teach me, Lord, to listen.
For at your Word my heart will sing and my soul will rejoice.

Melinda Mahand

Following His Example

A Moment to Pause

Set aside a few moments of your day to enjoy a brief time of solitude and contemplation. Find a quiet place to relax where there are no observers and where perhaps for a moment there will be no intruders. Invite the Lord to join you just now so that you may learn from his example.

As you slip away to enjoy this time to yourself, realize that you carry with you, each moment of every day, the imprints of people with whom you have shared significant relationships. These people have touched your life and thus become a part of it forever.

Think for a moment about the people who have made a difference in your life—parents, extended family members, friends, coworkers, neighbors, others. They have one thing in common. In every case, these people taught you something. Perhaps one taught you something about loving, another taught you something about working, and another taught you something about having fun.

Even if they were unaware of their influence on you, these people became your teachers. They taught you by example how to do the things you longed to do and how to be the person you longed to be. Their very lives became lessons you will never forget.

A teacher affects eternity; he can never tell
where his influence stops.
—Henry B. Adams

A Moment to Reflect

Likewise, God put you here to make a difference in someone's life. Do not imagine that your life is without powerful influence and great significance. You are teaching far more than mere subject matter. People are watching and people are learning from your example even at times when you are unaware.

Ask God to help you recognize that person who especially needs a teacher today. Invite him to work through you so that your touch on a person's life leaves God's imprint as well as yours. As you teach the students in your class and the other people around you, ask God to make your life a lesson they will never forget.

People watch us, see how we act in famine, in bereavement, in mortal distress; and in proportion as they see our integrity untouched, our prayer enlarged rather than diminished, our confidence established upon everlasting rocks, they may begin through our character to see our theology.... There comes a time when even a shattered life becomes an instrument of power.

ॐ

—Joseph Parker

Remember your leaders, who spoke the word of God to you. Consider the outcome of their way of life and imitate their faith.

Hebrews 13:7

A Moment to Refresh

Whatever is true, whatever is noble, whatever is right, whatever is pure, whatever is lovely, whatever is admirable—if anything is excellent or praiseworthy—think about such things. Whatever you have learned or received or heard from me, or seen in me—put it into practice. And the God of peace will be with you.

Philippians 4:8–9

Since we are surrounded by such a great cloud of witnesses, let us throw off everything that hinders and the sin that so easily entangles, and let us run with perseverance the race marked out for us. Let us fix our eyes on Jesus, the author and perfecter of our faith, who for the joy set before him endured the cross, scorning its shame, and sat down at the right hand of the throne of God.

Hebrews 12:1–2

Example is not the main thing in influencing others; it is the only thing.

~

—ALBERT SCHWEITZER

Come, my children, listen to me;
I will teach you the fear of the LORD.

Psalm 34:11

The LORD gives wisdom; From
His mouth come knowledge and
understanding. He stores up sound
wisdom for the upright; He is a
shield to those who walk in integrity.

Proverbs 2:6–7 NASB

Jesus said, "I have set you an example that
you should do as I have done for you."

John 13:15

Surely you desire truth in the inner parts;
you teach me wisdom in the inmost place,
O Lord.

Psalm 51:6

*The greatest power
for good is the
power of example.*

~

—AUTHOR
UNKNOWN

A Servant's Heart

A Moment to Pause Slip away to a place of peace and calmness today. Let your mind and body be refreshed as you enjoy the stillness. As you relax, let your imagination return for a moment to the place you left behind—the place where you teach.

Think about the tools you use to help your students learn. Perhaps you have access to videos, computer programs, and the Internet. Yet even in today's high-tech environment, a teacher's most common tools tend to be books, paper, and writing or drawing implements. These are humble tools for such an ambitious task. Yet humble tools accurately reflect the heart of a teacher, for a teacher's heart is a servant's heart.

Even the words people use to express thanks to you reflect the servant aspect of teaching. You are probably rarely praised for your vast knowledge or your skill at conveying concepts. Instead, students and parents remark: "Thank you for helping me." "Thank you for your time." "Thank you for listening."

Helping, availability, attentiveness—these are the deeds of a servant. Once again, they are humble deeds for such an ambitious task. Yet ultimately these are the deeds that make a difference in people's lives, for they open hearts and minds to receive teaching.

Always keep your eyes open for the little task,
because it is the little task that is
important to Jesus Christ.
—Albert Schweitzer

A Moment to Reflect Look to the life of Jesus for inspiration today. He, too, used humble tools and humble deeds to teach from a servant's heart. Yet no one who ever walked this earth has made a bigger difference in the hearts and minds and lives of people.

Be encouraged today by the knowledge that you, too, make a difference in people's lives. When you think your work has accomplished only a small amount in the life of a student, remember that even the greatest of achievements is actually a series of small victories, accomplished one at a time. Ask God to enable you to learn from him as you teach others and to serve him by serving others.

Christ has no body on earth but yours; yours are the only hands with which he can do his work, yours are the only feet with which he can go about the world, yours are the only eyes through which his compassion can shine forth upon a troubled world. Christ has no body now on earth but yours.

෨

—*Teresa of Avila*

Those who have served well gain an excellent standing and great assurance in their faith in Christ Jesus.

1 Timothy 3:13

A Moment to Refresh

Your attitude should be the same as that of Christ Jesus: Who, being in very nature God, did not consider equality with God something to be grasped, but made himself nothing, taking the very nature of a servant, being made in human likeness.

Philippians 2:5–7

Make a joyful noise unto the LORD, all ye lands. Serve the LORD with gladness: come before his presence with singing.

Psalm 100:1–2 KJV

A man's pride will bring him low, But a humble spirit will obtain honor.

Proverbs 29:23 NASB

No man was ever honored for what he received. Honor has been the reward for what he gave.

—Calvin Coolidge

Everyone who exalts himself will be humbled, and he who humbles himself will be exalted.

Luke 14:11

Jesus said, "Heaven will be like a man going on a journey, who called his servants and entrusted his property to them.... After a long time the master of those servants returned and settled accounts with them. The man who had received the five talents brought the other five. 'Master,' he said, 'you entrusted me with five talents. See, I have gained five more.' His master replied, 'Well done, good and faithful servant! You have been faithful with a few things; I will put you in charge of many things. Come and share your master's happiness!'"

Matthew 25:14, 19–20

The greatest reward for serving others is the satisfaction found in your own heart.

—Author Unknown

Mirror Images

A Moment to Pause Treat your face today to a bit of special pampering such as an exfoliating masque or a moisturizing cream. After all, your face has a rather demanding job. Seventy percent of communication is nonverbal, and much of that nonverbal communication takes place through the expressions of your face.

Look at your face in a mirror as you exfoliate or moisturize. Yours is the face students look to all day for encouragement and direction. Yours is the face that gives approval, warning, empathy, and acceptance. In addition, much that is in your mind and heart is reflected in your face.

Much that is in your mind and heart is also reflected in the lives of those you teach. After a while, you begin to see reflections of yourself in their attitudes, their actions, their beliefs, and their word choices. Sometimes you may even see one of your own facial expressions mirrored back to you!

Know, therefore, that your students are learning far more than academics. Much of what they discover about life, truth, and character they learn from a consistent daily relationship with you, their teacher. For what a teacher does, how a teacher thinks, and who a teacher is are the teacher's unspoken lessons.

Discipleship is more than getting to know what a teacher knows. It is getting to be what he is.
—Juan Carlos Ortiz

A Moment to Reflect

Thank God today for the great opportunity you have been given to affect the future of the students you teach. Ask him to work through you to prepare them for the destiny he has designed. Dedicate yourself to working together with God to mold the students' minds, chisel their character, and inspire their spirits.

Then spend some time learning from the Lord today. As the psalmist said, "Look to the LORD and his strength; seek his face always" (Psalm 105:4). Invite him to teach you his truth and his ways so that your life may be a reflection of him to the students who watch you each day.

If a child lives with fairness, he learns what justice is.
If a child lives with honesty, he learns what truth is.
If a child lives with sincerity, he learns to have faith
in himself and those around him.
If a child lives with love, he learns that the world is a
wonderful place to live in.

～

—AUTHOR UNKNOWN

17

A student is not above his teacher, but everyone who is fully trained will be like his teacher.

Luke 6:40

A Moment to Refresh

Since my youth, O God, you have taught me, and to this day I declare your marvelous deeds. Even when I am old and gray, do not forsake me, O God, till I declare your power to the next generation, your might to all who are to come.

Psalm 71:17–18

It is Christ whom we proclaim, warning everyone and teaching everyone in all wisdom, so that we may present everyone mature in Christ. For this I toil and struggle with all the energy that he powerfully inspires within me.

Colossians 1:28–29 NRSV

Pay attention to the sayings of the wise; apply your heart to what I teach, for it is pleasing when you keep them in your heart and have all of them ready on your lips. So that your trust may be in the LORD, I teach you today, even you.

Psalm 22:17–19

Children have more need of models than of critics.

—JOSEPH JOUBERT

Listen, my people, to my teaching,
and pay attention to what I say.
I am going to use wise sayings
and explain mysteries from the past,
things we have heard and known,
things that our ancestors told us.
We will not keep them from our children;
we will tell the next generation
about the LORD's power and his great
deeds and the wonderful things he has done.
                                    Psalm 78:1–4 GNT

Let the word of Christ dwell in you richly
as you teach and admonish one another
with all wisdom, and as you sing psalms,
hymns and spiritual songs with gratitude in
your hearts to God. And whatever you do,
whether in word or deed, do it all in the
name of the Lord Jesus, giving thanks to
God the Father through him.
                                    Colossians 3:16–17

*There is just one
way to train up a
child in the way he
should go and that
is to travel that way
yourself.*

—ABRAHAM LINCOLN

Invest Your Time Wisely

A Moment to Pause   Let the tasks that crowd your schedule and consume your time stand aside today as you enjoy the luxury of stillness and solitude. Realize that such moments are not a waste of time. They are, rather, an investment that enables you to better use the rest of your day.

The use and measurement of time is of supreme interest these days. Stop watches, wristwatches, and alarm clocks keep you in constant awareness of every passing second. Your interest is not misplaced, however, for the Creator himself made the sun, moon, and stars to serve as tools for measuring time (Genesis 1:14).

Yet despite these tools of measurement, you can neither stop time nor save it. No bank exists where you can hoard time in case you need more of it in the future. You cannot borrow time if you need more of it now; you cannot undo an unwise investment of time made in the past; you cannot count on being able to invest time in the future. You have only this day to invest now and to invest well.

What we weave in time we wear in eternity.
—John Charles Ryle

A Moment to Reflect

How do you choose to invest your time when every moment is precious? Where can you find the strength to schedule your day according to your chosen priorities rather than to succumb to the tyranny of the urgent?

Once again, you can go to the Lord for help and for answers. After all, he created time, and he has a plan for its use in your life. He cares about the pressures and the stresses of your day. Ask him to show you those things he has called you to do. He will help you recognize which tasks to gladly accept and which ones to turn down without regret or guilt.

I would the precious time redeem,
And longer live for this alone,
To spend, and to be spent, for them
Who have not yet my Savior known;
Fully on these my mission prove,
And only breathe, to breathe Thy love.

✂

—Charles Wesley

May the Lord of peace himself give you peace
at all times and in every way. The Lord be with
all of you.

2 Thessalonians 3:16

A Moment to Refresh

Your eyes saw my unformed body.
All the days ordained for me
were written in your book
before one of them came to be.
How precious to me are your thoughts, O God!

Psalm 139:16–17

There is a time for everything,
and a season for every activity under heaven:
a time to be born and a time to die,
a time to plant and a time to uproot,
a time to kill and a time to heal,
a time to tear down and a time to build,
a time to weep and a time to laugh,
a time to mourn and a time to dance.

Ecclesiastes 3:1–4

God is able to make all grace abound to you, so
that in all things at all times, having all that you
need, you will abound in every good work.

2 Corinthians 9:8

Life is too short for us to do everything we want to do; but it is long enough for us to do everything God wants us to do.

~

Teach us to number our days, that we may apply our hearts unto wisdom.

Psalm 90:12 KJV

*God is wise and powerful!
Praise him forever and ever.
He controls the times and the seasons;
he makes and unmakes kings;
it is he who gives wisdom and
understanding.*

Daniel 2:20–21 GNT

*My times are in your hands, LORD;
deliver me from my enemies
and from those who pursue me....
How great is your goodness,
which you have stored up for
those who fear you, which you
bestow in the sight of men
on those who take refuge in you.*

Psalm 31:15, 19

*Take my life,
and let it be
Consecrated, Lord,
to Thee;
Take my moments
and my days,
Let them flow in
ceaseless praise.*

~

—FRANCES RIDLEY
HAVERGAL

God Knows and Loves You

A Moment to Pause

Has anyone loved you today? Has anyone known your nerves are frazzled, your body is tired, and your feet are sore—and yet still found you lovable? Yes, someone has. God has. Retreat now to a place of quietness, a place where you can pause in his presence and rest in his love.

As you spend these quiet moments with God, recognize that his love is essentially different from the love of your students, your friends, and even your family members. Although these people know your quirks, your preferences, your habits, and your dreams, God knows you even more intimately. He knows your thoughts, your secrets, your motives, and your deepest desires. He knows what you are going to say before you say it, and he knows what you need before you ask him. God knows every minor detail of your daily life right down to the number of hairs on your head at any given moment.

God knows you better than you know yourself. The wondrous news is that he also loves you better than you love yourself. God knows you completely, and still he loves you. This description is the essence of unconditional love.

God loves you as if you are the only person in the world.
—Augustine of Hippo

24

A Moment to Reflect

Take a moment to read the verses on the following pages, for they describe God's unconditional love for you. Notice that God does not change you and thus make it possible for him to love you. Neither does he love you solely for the purpose of changing you. He just loves you as you are, unconditionally. Period.

Yet God's unconditional love is transforming, for his love makes you alive in the places where once you were dead. Let God's love transform your heart and your life today. He offers you an intimate relationship of unconditional, unchanging love, right here on earth, right now, today and every day.

Some of us believe that God is almighty and may do everything, and that he is all-wisdom and can do everything; but that he is all-love and wishes to do everything—there we stop short. It is this ignorance, it seems to me, that hinders most of God's lovers.

—JULIAN OF NORWICH

God demonstrates his own love for us in this:
While we were still sinners, Christ died for us.

Romans 5:8

A Moment to Refresh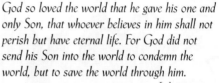

God so loved the world that he gave his one and only Son, that whoever believes in him shall not perish but have eternal life. For God did not send his Son into the world to condemn the world, but to save the world through him.

John 3:16–17

Because of his great love for us, God, who is rich in mercy, made us alive with Christ even when we were dead in transgressions—it is by grace you have been saved.

Ephesians 2:4–5

We know and rely on the love God has for us. God is love. Whoever lives in love lives in God, and God in him.... We love because he first loved us.

1 John 4:16, 19

However devoted you are to God, you can be sure he is immeasurably more devoted to you.

ॐ

—MEISTER ECKHART

When the kindness and love of God our Savior appeared, he saved us, not because of righteous things we had done, but because of his mercy. He saved us through the washing of rebirth and renewal by the Holy Spirit, whom he poured out on us generously through Jesus Christ our Savior, so that, having been justified by his grace, we might become heirs having the hope of eternal life.

Titus 3:4–7

God does not treat us as our sins deserve or repay us according to our iniquities.
For as high as the heavens are above the earth, so great is his love for those who fear him; as far as the east is from the west, so far has he removed our transgressions from us. As a father has compassion on his children, so the LORD has compassion on those who fear him.

Psalm 103:10–13

The love of God is like the Amazon River flowing down to water one daisy.

ॐ

—AUTHOR UNKNOWN

God Is with You

A Moment to Pause Allow yourself some time to lean back just now and let the burdens and the tensions of the day drift away. Feel your muscles relax and your mind ease as you enjoy a few moments of peaceful relaxation. Welcome God into these moments of retreat.

Teachers are often tired and tense at the end of the day because of the many hours you spend taking care of the needs of others. You complete piles of paperwork for the office staff, you answer endless questions for parents, you offer sympathetic help and advice for other teachers, and you provide everything from a tissue or a pat on the back to a private tutor for your students!

Yes, some days it seems that every person who enters your presence needs something from you, and so you look forward to simply spending some time alone. Yet when you enter the house and set down the book bags or satchels that form your physical burdens, you sense a great need to let go of the burdens of your soul as well. You long not for absolute solitude, but rather for a presence who will simply be with you, to listen, to care, and to lessen the load that you carry.

We may accustom ourselves to a continual conversation with God, with freedom and in simplicity. We need only to recognize God intimately present with us, to address ourselves to Him every moment.
—*Brother Lawrence*

A Moment to Reflect

Today, whether your heart is desperate or simply weary, whether your day has been difficult or simply demanding, whether your need is for a protector and provider or simply for a friend, God is there. The truth is, in fact, that God is always with you. He is with you even in the day-to-day tasks of straightening a classroom, grading a paper, guiding a student, or working with a parent.

Turn to God today when you need someone to listen and to care. Then begin to practice being consciously aware of him each moment of the day, for his presence is one that will give, renew, restore, and make you whole.

Would you like me to tell you what supported me through all the years of exile among a people whose language I could not understand, and whose attitude to me was always uncertain and often hostile? It was this, "Lo, I am with you always, even unto the end of the world." On these words I staked everything, and they never failed.

—David Livingstone

"My Presence will go with you, and I will give you rest," says the LORD.

Exodus 33:14

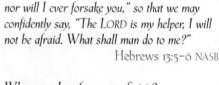

A Moment to Refresh

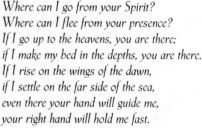

God Himself has said, "I will never desert you, nor will I ever forsake you," so that we may confidently say, "The LORD is my helper, I will not be afraid. What shall man do to me?"

Hebrews 13:5–6 NASB

Where can I go from your Spirit?
Where can I flee from your presence?
If I go up to the heavens, you are there;
if I make my bed in the depths, you are there.
If I rise on the wings of the dawn,
if I settle on the far side of the sea,
even there your hand will guide me,
your right hand will hold me fast.

Psalm 139:7–10

Do not fear, for I am with you;
do not be dismayed, for I am your God.
I will strengthen you and help you;
I will uphold you with my righteous right hand.

Isaiah 41:10

God is not an idea, or a definition that we have committed to memory, he is a presence which we experience in our hearts.

❧

—LOUIS EVELY

You have made known to me the path of life, O LORD; you will fill me with joy in your presence, with eternal pleasures at your right hand.

Psalm 16:11

From one ancestor God made all nations to inhabit the whole earth, and he allotted the times of their existence and the boundaries of the places where they would live, so that they would search for God and perhaps grope for him and find him—though indeed he is not far from each one of us.

Acts 17:26–27 NRSV

Great is the LORD, and greatly to be praised: he also is to be feared above all gods.... Glory and honour are in his presence; strength and gladness are in his place.

1 Chronicles 16:25, 27 KJV

God is above, presiding; beneath, sustaining; within, filling.

❧

—HILDEBERT OF LAVARDIN

One Muscle That Shouldn't Flex

A Moment to Pause

Sometimes a warm cup of your favorite coffee or tea or a tall, cool glass of water with lemon is a great way to begin soothing your throat, calming your nerves, and encouraging your muscles to take it easy for a while. Whatever your favorite comforting concoction may be, take a few minutes to prepare and enjoy one now. Relish these moments of quiet relaxation while you enjoy this small reprieve.

As you take time to sip your refreshment, ponder the many positive ways you used your mouth on this day. Perhaps you began the day distributing kisses to family members. Perhaps you greeted sleepy students with a welcoming smile. You most likely had several occasions when you used your words to encourage, to praise, to guide, to counsel, or to console. Yes, your mouth has the power to affect great good in the lives of others.

Yet just as with any powerful tool, the mouth has the potential to be misused as well. The shears that prune a tree can also puncture its fruit. The hoe that cultivates a garden can also cleave its produce. The mouth that has the power to prompt, promote, and praise can also paralyze, poison, and profane.

Converse as those would who know that God hears.
—Tertullian

A Moment to Reflect Stop now to thank God for the privilege of a teaching position that allows you to influence and bless others with your words. Ask him to help you continue to use your mouth to build up and not to tear down, to determine destinies and not to destroy dreams.

Also spend some time just now listening to God's words to you and incorporating their truth into your life. His words above all others have the power to affect great good on your behalf. For in the Bible God has proclaimed words of promise and hope, love and salvation, wisdom and strength for your heart today.

Cold words freeze people, and hot words scorch them, and bitter words make them bitter, and wrathful words make them wrathful. Kind words also produce their image on men's souls; and a beautiful image it is. They smooth, and quiet, and comfort the hearer.

—BLAISE PASCAL

A man of knowledge uses words with restraint,
and a man of understanding is even-tempered.
Even a fool is thought wise if he keeps silent,
and discerning if he holds his tongue.

Proverbs 17:27–28

A Moment to Refresh

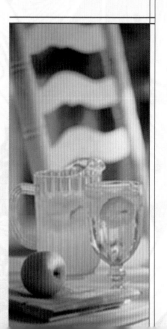

Pleasant words are a honeycomb,
sweet to the soul and healing to the bones.

Proverbs 16:24

May the words of my mouth and the meditation
of my heart be pleasing in your sight,
O LORD, my Rock and my Redeemer.

Psalm 19:14

Live in harmony with one another; be
sympathetic, love as brothers, be compassionate
and humble. Do not repay evil with evil or
insult with insult, but with blessing, because to
this you were called so that you
may inherit a blessing.

1 Peter 3:8–9

Kind words are the music of the world.

⁓

—FREDERICK WILLIAM FABER

May our Lord Jesus Christ himself and God our Father, who loved us and through grace gave us eternal comfort and good hope, comfort your hearts and strengthen them in every good work and word.

2 Thessalonians 2:16–17 NRSV

*Listen, O heavens, and I will speak;
hear, O earth, the words of my mouth.
Let my teaching fall like rain
and my words descend like dew,
like showers on new grass,
like abundant rain on tender plants.
I will proclaim the name of the LORD.
Oh, praise the greatness of our God!*

Deuteronomy 32:1–3

Encouragement costs you nothing to give, but it is priceless to receive.

⁓

—AUTHOR UNKNOWN

Choosing to Forgive

A Moment to Pause

Just now, allow yourself a small reprieve from today's full schedule. Refresh your mind and heart with a few minutes of reflection. Select a spot where you can view the wonders of the natural world outdoors. As you quietly rest, consider the ways in which choosing to forgive resembles the many regularly occurring cycles of nature outside.

Every twenty-four hours, we experience the cycle of day and night. Once a year, we observe the complete cycle of the seasons from fall and winter to spring and summer. Even in an insect as seemingly insignificant as a caterpillar, we notice the change from a pupa to a chrysalis to an adult butterfly, which will begin the cycle again.

These cycles are so familiar to our eyes and to our minds that we often let them pass without acknowledgment. Yet when we pause to ponder their message, we begin to realize that they illustrate a beautiful message about God's goodness to us. Through the twenty-four-hour day, we discover that although there is darkness, there is also light. In the seasons we find that although there is death, there is also life. From the simple caterpillar, we are reminded that although there are endings, there are also new beginnings.

To forgive is to set a prisoner free and discover the prisoner was you.
—Author Unknown

A Moment to Reflect God knew that His people would need opportunities for recovery and renewal as well. He knew that as we learn to live in relationships with one another, we sometimes experience troubling misunderstandings, difficult arguments, poor attitudes, and unkind words. Yet God did not want our relationships to forever remain in places of darkness, death, and endings. So God demonstrated the power of forgiveness. He understood that this dynamic force brings light, life, and new beginnings to relationships.

Who do you need to forgive today? Ask God for the grace to do so now. Amazingly, forgiveness will bring as much healing and renewal for your own heart as it does for the heart of the one to whom you offer it.

We all have some weakness, some point of failure, some signature of the dust. Blessed are they who have great, generous, royal, divine hearts. The more a man can forgive, the more does he resemble God.

༃

—Joseph Parker

37

"Lord, how often shall my brother sin against me and I forgive him? Up to seven times?" Jesus said to him, "I do not say to you, up to seven times, but up to seventy times seven."

Matthew 18:21–22 NASB

A Moment to Refresh

Jesus said, "Be merciful, just as your Father is merciful. Do not judge, and you will not be judged. Do not condemn, and you will not be condemned. Forgive, and you will be forgiven. Give, and it will be given to you. A good measure, pressed down, shaken together and running over, will be poured into your lap. For with the measure you use, it will be measured to you."

Luke 6:36–38

As God's chosen people, holy and dearly loved, clothe yourselves with compassion, kindness, humility, gentleness and patience. Bear with each other and forgive whatever grievances you may have against one another. Forgive as the Lord forgave you.

Colossians 3:12–13

Forgiveness is man's deepest need and highest achievement.

—HORACE BUSHNELL

If you forgive others the wrongs they have done to you, your Father in heaven will also forgive you.

Matthew 6:14 GNT

Who is a God like you,
who pardons sin and forgives the
transgression of the remnant of his
inheritance? You do not stay angry
forever but delight to show mercy.
You will again have compassion on us;
you will tread our sins underfoot
and hurl all our iniquities into the
depths of the sea.

Micah 7:18–19

Blessed are the merciful,
for they will be shown mercy.

Matthew 5:7

He that cannot forgive others breaks the bridge over which he must pass himself; for every man has need to be forgiven.

—THOMAS FULLER

Listen Closely

A Moment to Pause Wherever you are right now, suspend your busy thoughts and activities and spend a few moments simply listening. Remain still and quiet as you relax and listen. Listen closely.

What do you hear? Do you hear air systems blowing? People talking? Machines running? Cars traveling? Footsteps hurrying?

Many of the sounds that surround us each day are auditory reminders of our fast-paced, ever-changing, ever-on-the-go society. In our modern world, the ability to simply listen attentively is a rare trait, yet it definitely has its rewards. Quietly listening to another person often provides new insight, heightens awareness, or enhances understanding. Remember, for instance, a time when you stood behind a struggling student and softly offered guidance. Consider the benefits that student received when she listened carefully to your words. You not only provided the help she needed to turn from her error, but you also revealed the correct way for her to proceed.

Likewise, God offers guidance that greatly benefits those who choose to listen. Much like your words to a student, God longs for his words to be heard as far more than a critical analysis of your performance. He desires that his words gently turn you away from error and guide you along the right path for your life.

Blessed are those who listen, for they shall learn.
—Author Unknown

40

A Moment to Reflect

Although you hear God with your heart rather than with your physical ears, you must still come to Him prepared to listen. So pause for a moment to listen again just now. Can you hear God speaking to you?

The psalms in the Bible are a good place to begin discovering God's words for your life. Spend a few minutes reading them today. Within their pages you will find encouragement, guidance, strength, comfort, and hope. As you read, ask God to talk to you personally. Then prayerfully listen for his voice. He is always faithful to speak to those who listen.

How, Lord, do I listen? For your voice speaks
in ocean waves as they crash to the shore.
How, Lord, do I listen? For your voice speaks
in thunder blasts as heavy rain showers pour.
Teach me, Lord, to listen. For I am waiting eagerly;
I long to hear your voice.
Teach me, Lord, to listen.
For at your Word my heart will sing
and my soul will rejoice.

—MELINDA MAHAND

I will listen to what God the LORD will say;
he promises peace to his people.

Psalm 85:8

A Moment to Refresh

Whoever listens to me will live in safety
and be at ease, without fear of harm.

Proverbs 1:33

If you wander off the road to the right or the
left, you will hear God's voice behind you
saying, "Here is the road. Follow it."

Isaiah 30:21 GNT

Let me hear Your lovingkindness in the
morning;
For I trust in You, O LORD;
Teach me the way in which I should walk;
For to You I lift up my soul.

Psalm 143:8 NASB

He whose ear listens to the life-giving reproof
Will dwell among the wise. He who neglects
discipline despises himself, But he who listens to
reproof acquires understanding.

Proverbs 15:31-32 NASB

Speak, Lord, in the stillness,
While I wait on Thee;
Hushed my heart to listen
In expectancy.

—C. MARY CRAWFORD

Jesus said, "I tell you the truth, whoever hears my word and believes him who sent me has eternal life and will not be condemned; he has crossed over from death to life."

John 5:24

The heart of the discerning
acquires knowledge;
the ears of the wise seek it out.

Proverbs 18:15

Jesus said, "Here I am! I stand at the door and knock. If anyone hears my voice and opens the door, I will come in and eat with him, and he with me."

Revelation 3:20

Devout meditation on the Word is more important to soul-health even than prayer. It is more needful for you to hear God's words than that God should hear yours, though the one will always lead to the other.

—F. B. MEYER

Power to Rule the Stars

A Moment to Pause This evening sit outdoors for a while and enjoy the spectacular view of the stars in the nighttime sky. Quietly gaze as far as you can into the heavens and consider God's all-powerful hand displayed in his universe. Rest for a few moments as you enjoy the awesome sight.

Did you know that on a clear night it is possible to see about five thousand stars in the sky? Although impressive, this number is only a minute fraction of the stars in the galaxy. In fact, scientists explain that the Milky Way galaxy contains hundreds of billions of individual stars. As amazing as that number seems, it is once again only a minute fraction of the innumerable stars among the countless galaxies in the universe.

Do you have trouble even beginning to conceive that number of stars? The thought of trying to actually count them boggles the mind. Yet the Bible says God not only numbers the stars, but he knows them individually and names them as well. God knows the features that distinguish one of his stars from another as intimately as you know the features that distinguish one of your students from another. As David the psalm writer said, "Such knowledge is too wonderful for me; It is too high, I cannot attain to it" (Psalm 139:6 NASB).

God writes the gospel not in the Bible alone, but on trees, and flowers, and clouds, and stars.
—Martin Luther

A Moment to Reflect

If God in his wisdom calls each star by name and knows precisely how to care for it in the heavenly sphere, doesn't he also know how to best care for you? God does not simply look down upon the earth and see an indistinct, huddled mass of humanity. Rather, he sees and recognizes you as an individual. In fact, he calls you by name. He knows you intimately, and he cares for you personally.

You can trust the Lord's wisdom for your life. As the stars do not fail the nighttime, so he will not fail you.

He formed the stars,
those heavenly flames,
He counts their number,
calls their names;
His wisdom's vast,
and knows no bound,
A deep where all
our thoughts are drowned.

—ISAAC WATTS

45

*He determines the number of the stars
and calls them each by name.
Great is our LORD and mighty in power;
his understanding has no limit.*

Psalm 147:4–5

A Moment to Refresh

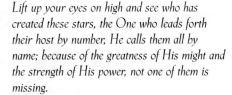

*Lift up your eyes on high and see who has
created these stars, the One who leads forth
their host by number, He calls them all by
name; because of the greatness of His might and
the strength of His power, not one of them is
missing.*

Isaiah 40:26 NASB

*By the word of the LORD were the
heavens made, their starry host by the
breath of his mouth.*

Psalm 33:6

*The LORD's unfailing love and mercy still
continue, fresh as the morning, as sure as
the sunrise. The LORD is all I have,
and so in him I put my hope.*

Lamentations 3:22–24 GNT

The universe is but one vast symbol of God.

—THOMAS CARLYLE

*How great is the love the Father has
lavished on us, that we should be called
children of God! And that is what we are!*
1 John 3:1

*Give thanks to the Lord of lords:
His love endures forever.
to him who alone does great wonders,
His love endures forever.
who...made the heavens,
His love endures forever.
who spread out the earth upon the waters,
His love endures forever.
who made the great lights—
His love endures forever.
the sun to govern the day,
His love endures forever.
the moon and stars to govern the night;
His love endures forever.*
Psalm 136:3–9

*The more we learn
about the wonders
of our universe, the
more clearly we are
going to perceive the
hand of God.*

—FRANK BORMAN

Just Ask

A Moment to Pause

Whether you are preparing to begin your day or finally drawing it to a close, take time to spend a few minutes in quiet meditation. Recognize that God is with you, ready to hear the concerns on your heart, ready to provide answers to any questions troubling your soul.

As a teacher, you have a certain knack for asking questions as well as for answering them. But the types of questions you usually ask are ones designed to help your students, not questions that confess your own need for help. You most likely possess an inner drive to discover information and figure out problems. That drive is part of what distinguishes you as an effective teacher. Yet that same drive may often make you hesitant to ask for assistance, for you want to be able to find your own answers and resolve your own problems. You may become like some of your students—either too embarrassed or too stubborn to ask for help.

Yet even the best teachers encounter questions that they cannot answer, questions that require more than human wisdom or human reasoning to resolve, questions that require an all-knowing God.

Prayer can do anything God can do.
—E. M. Bounds

A Moment to Reflect

God is waiting for you to turn to him with your questions. He wants to be the provider of answers for you as well as be the provider for every need in your life. Although God knows your questions and your needs before you ask, he will often wait to answer until you turn to him in prayer. Prayer not only demonstrates your awareness of your need for God, but it also builds and strengthens your relationship with him, just as communication builds and strengthens any relationship.

What are the questions that have disquieted your thoughts and emotions today? Talk to God about each one of them. He is waiting to hear and to answer. All you have to do is ask.

There is no thought, feeling, yearning or desire, however low, trifling, or vulgar we may deem it, which, if it affects our real interest or happiness, we may not lay before God and be sure of sympathy. His nature is such that our often coming does not tire him. The whole burden of the whole life of every man may be rolled on to God and not weary him, though it has wearied the man.

—Henry Ward Beecher

49

Know that the LORD has set apart the godly for himself; the LORD will hear when I call to him.

Psalm 4:3

A Moment to Refresh

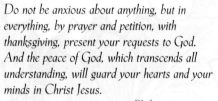

Do not be anxious about anything, but in everything, by prayer and petition, with thanksgiving, present your requests to God. And the peace of God, which transcends all understanding, will guard your hearts and your minds in Christ Jesus.

Philippians 4:6–7

Is there anyone among you who, if your child asks for bread, will give a stone? Or if the child asks for a fish, will give a snake? If you then, who are evil, know how to give good gifts to your children, how much more will your Father in heaven give good things to those who ask him!

Matthew 7:9–11 NRSV

He can give only according to His might; therefore He always gives more than we ask for.

❧

—MARTIN LUTHER

If any of you lacks wisdom, he should ask God, who gives generously to all without finding fault, and it will be given to him. But when he asks, he must believe and not doubt, because he who doubts is like a wave of the sea, blown and tossed by the wind.

James 1:5–6

Jesus said, "Your Father knows what you need before you ask him."

Matthew 6:8

I urge, then, first of all, that requests, prayers, intercession and thanksgiving be made for everyone...that we may live peaceful and quiet lives in all godliness and holiness. This is good, and pleases God our Savior, who wants all men to be saved and to come to a knowledge of the truth.

1 Timothy 2:1–4

I live in the spirit of prayer. I pray as I walk about, when I lie down and when I rise up. And the answers are always coming.

❧

—GEORGE MULLER

Working with Your Heart

A Moment to Pause Reward yourself for a job well done by taking time to relax and unwind. Look slowly around the room. What small items do you see? Consider how important those items are to your daily life, whether for sentimental or utilitarian reasons. You will find that many small things make a big difference. Now think for a moment of the small tasks you performed today, tasks such as affirming a student, grading a paper, or explaining a concept. These tasks, though small in nature, can make a big difference in people's lives when you work not just with your hands and mind, but also with your heart.

Recall the small tasks Jesus performed, tasks such as washing his disciples' feet, talking to a woman by a well, and cooking fish on the seashore. These small tasks became lessons that had great impact on people's lives.

Jesus understood that his work was God's work. He even said his life's sustenance was "to do the will of Him who sent Me and to accomplish His work" (John 4:34 NASB). This outlook transformed Jesus' tasks into works from the heart, works with purpose. This outlook is one you can share.

Far and away the best prize that life offers is the chance to work hard at work worth doing.
—*Theodore Roosevelt*

A Moment to Reflect

God designed work to be an undertaking that provides mental, physical, and spiritual satisfaction. By committing your work to the Lord, you allow him to work in you and through you as you carry out your daily tasks. Your work then becomes his work, and his work makes a difference in the lives of people it touches.

Your job will always have its challenges and disappointments, of course. When you commit your work to the Lord, you can entrust to him the troubling aspects as well. Ask him now to renew you and guide you each day as you serve him through your work.

He who labours as he prays
lifts up his heart to God
with his hands.

—Saint Bernard of Clairvaux

53

Whatever you do, work at it with all your heart, as working for the Lord, not for men, since you know that you will receive an inheritance from the Lord as a reward. It is the Lord Christ you are serving.

Colossians 3:23–24

A Moment to Refresh

She considers a field and buys it; out of her earnings she plants a vineyard. She sets about her work vigorously; her arms are strong for her tasks. She sees that her trading is profitable, and her lamp does not go out at night.

Proverbs 31:16–18

Let us not become weary in doing good, for at the proper time we will reap a harvest if we do not give up. Therefore, as we have opportunity, let us do good to all people, especially to those who belong to the family of believers.

Galatians 6:9–10

Obey them not only to win their favor when their eye is on you but like slaves of Christ, doing the will of God from your heart. Serve wholeheartedly, as if you were serving the Lord, not men, because you know that the Lord will reward everyone for whatever good he does.

Ephesians 6:6–8

One may do much [work] or one may do little; it is all one, provided he directs his heart to heaven.

❧

—Berakoth Jewish Reform Prayer

Do everything without complaining or arguing, so that you may become blameless and pure, children of God without fault in a crooked and depraved generation, in which you shine like stars in the universe as you hold out the word of life.

Philippians 2:14–16

I thank Christ Jesus our Lord, who has given me strength, that he considered me faithful, appointing me to his service.

1 Timothy 1:12

Steadfast love belongs to you, O Lord. For you repay to all according to their work.

Psalm 62:12 NRSV

All a man's ways seem innocent to him, but motives are weighed by the LORD. Commit to the LORD whatever you do, and your plans will succeed.

Proverbs 16:2–3

I long to accomplish a great and noble task; but it is my chief duty to accomplish small tasks as if they were great and noble.

❧

—Helen Keller

Seasoned Speech

A Moment to Pause

Do you need a change of pace today—a time to slow down and gather your thoughts? If so, pause now and allow yourself a few moments of stillness to quiet your mind. As the day's tensions begin to ease, think back on your day and recall any uplifting words others shared with you. Perhaps you heard words of encouragement, words of affirmation, or words of appreciation. Thank God just now for the people who blessed you with their words.

The Bible encourages you to use words carefully. In fact, Scripture advises that you season your speech as if with salt. Although this instruction sounds odd at first, it is actually quite enlightening. The same salt that can preserve meat also has the power to disintegrate the concrete of a sidewalk. The salt that enhances the flavor of food when used sparingly can also, when used liberally, make food unpalatable.

Likewise, words have the power to preserve a person or to destroy, to enhance or to tear down. Christians must be as careful about the way they use words, for both salt and words bear an impact out of proportion to their size.

Our words are a faithful index of
the state of our souls.
—Francis de Sales

A Moment to Reflect

Your words are like salt. They are powerful tools with the potential to do great good or great harm. Spend a few minutes today measuring your words by the guidelines in the verses on the following pages. In what areas do you need to use your words more carefully or more sparingly? In what instances have your words been filled with grace? Do you speak the very words of God, and do the words of your mouth please the Lord? Do your words echo kindness?

Ask the Lord to help you be mindful of your words each day so that you may be careful to preserve and enhance the minds and spirits of others.

The wise in heart are called discerning, and pleasant words promote instruction. Understanding is a fountain of life to those who have it, but folly brings punishment to fools. A wise man's heart guides his mouth, and his lips promote instruction.

✣

—PROVERBS 16:21–23

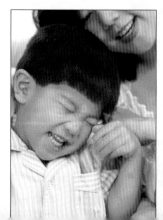

He who restrains his words has knowledge,
and he who has a cool spirit is a man of
understanding.

Proverbs 17:27 NASB

A Moment to Refresh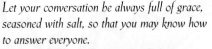

Let your conversation be always full of grace,
seasoned with salt, so that you may know how
to answer everyone.

Colossians 4:6

Each one should use whatever gift he has
received to serve others, faithfully administering
God's grace in its various forms. If anyone
speaks, he should do it as one speaking the very
words of God. If anyone serves, he should do it
with the strength God provides, so that in all
things God may be praised through Jesus
Christ. To him be the glory and the power for
ever and ever.

1 Peter 4:10–11

An evil man is trapped by his sinful talk, but a
righteous man escapes trouble. From the fruit of
his lips a man is filled with good things as
surely as the work of his hands rewards him.

Proverbs 12:13–14

Kind words can be short and easy to speak, but their echoes are truly endless.

ॐ

—MOTHER TERESA

David sang, May the words of my mouth and the meditation of my heart be pleasing in your sight, O LORD, my Rock and my Redeemer.

Psalm 19:14

Do not lie to each other, since you have taken off your old self with its practices and have put on the new self, which is being renewed in knowledge in the image of its Creator.

Colossians 3:9–10

Good words are worth much and cost little.

ॐ

—GEORGE HERBERT

From the fruit of his mouth a man's stomach is filled; with the harvest from his lips he is satisfied. The tongue has the power of life and death, and those who love it will eat its fruit.

Proverbs 18:20–21

Go to the Source

A Moment to Pause

Invite God to speak to your heart today. He alone is the source of all understanding and wisdom. Enjoy being with him as you ponder the words of today's meditation.

What are the steps you would take if you were interested in learning about a person? You might read a biography of the person or read books written by her. If she were still living, you might follow the events of her life through newspapers, magazines, television, and Web news. Perhaps you might have opportunity to talk to people who know her. Yet regardless of how much you learned *about* her, you still could not say you *know* her. Knowing someone requires going to the source—the person herself—and spending time together, talking openly and sharing honestly. Truly knowing a person requires that you have a relationship with that person.

In much the same way, you cannot know wisdom by reading quotations and Bible verses about it. Neither can you know wisdom by listening to or talking to wise people. Wisdom is more than just the acquisition of information and knowledge. Wisdom comes only through intimate discourse with the source—the Lord God himself.

I find the Scriptures declare all wisdom
to be a divine gift.
—Clement of Rome

A Moment to Reflect

*I*nterestingly, the book of Proverbs uses the creative approach of depicting wisdom as a woman speaking to humanity. Perhaps the Lord chose this depiction of wisdom as a person because coming to *know* wisdom is the result and the sign of a relationship. In order for a person to know true wisdom, that person must first know the Lord.

Are there problems or dilemmas in your life that require wisdom to resolve? Put yourself in a position to learn from God today. Spend time talking with and listening to him. Commit to live out the truths he reveals to your heart, for then you will begin to know true wisdom. Go to the source.

Give me, O Lord, heavenly wisdom, that I may learn to seek Thee above all things and to find Thee; to relish Thee above all things and to love Thee; and to understand all other things, even as they are, according to the order of Thy wisdom.

—Thomas à Kempis

61

The way to become wise is to honor the LORD.
Psalm 111:10 GNT

A Moment to Refresh

Wisdom is supreme; therefore get wisdom. Though it cost all you have, get understanding. Esteem her, and she will exalt you; embrace her, and she will honor you. She will set a garland of grace on your head and present you with a crown of splendor.

Proverbs 4:7–9

Who is wise and understanding among you? Let him show it by his good life, by deeds done in the humility that comes from wisdom.... But the wisdom that comes from heaven is first of all pure; then peace-loving, considerate, submissive, full of mercy and good fruit, impartial and sincere.

James 3:13, 17

Only the wise know what things really mean. Wisdom makes them smile and makes their frowns disappear.

Ecclesiastes 8:1 GNT

Wisdom is the right use of knowledge. To know is not to be wise... There is no fool so great as a knowing fool. But to know how to use knowledge is to have wisdom.

—CHARLES HADDON SPURGEON

Blessed is the man who finds wisdom, the man who gains understanding, for she is more profitable than silver and yields better returns than gold. She is more precious than rubies; nothing you desire can compare with her. Long life is in her right hand; in her left hand are riches and honor. Her ways are pleasant ways, and all her paths are peace. She is a tree of life to those who embrace her; those who lay hold of her will be blessed.

Proverbs 3:13–18

Wisdom is proud
that he has learned
so much;
Wisdom is humble
that he knows no
more.

—WILLIAM COWPER

Where can wisdom be found? Where does understanding dwell? Man does not comprehend its worth; it cannot be found in the land of the living.... It cannot be bought with the finest gold, nor can its price be weighed in silver.... God understands the way to it and he alone knows where it dwells.

Job 28:12–13, 15, 23

God Is Your Strength

A Moment to Pause

After a busy day of teaching, you may feel more than tired—you may actually feel weak. Your weakness just now is God's opportunity to display his strength in you. Allow him to refresh and restore your soul as you spend time with him.

Do the challenges you face each day in your personal life and in the lives of your students loom before you, intimidating and instilling fear? Do you sometimes feel weak or even paralyzed as a result? God has good news for you today: looks can be deceiving. What you may perceive as a difficult challenge or even an impossible challenge, God perceives as an incredible opportunity. For when God desires to display his power, he works through a Christian who chooses to confront the difficult. And when God wants to work a miracle, he works through a Christian who chooses to confront the impossible.

Today God invites you to stop being intimidated by the power of the obstacle and start believing in the power of his strength and will. Imagine what God can do as you begin to focus on the important, the imposing, and the impossible and trust him to do mighty acts through you in each of those areas.

When God is our strength, it is strength indeed;
when our strength is our own,
it is only weakness.
—Augustine of Hippo

A Moment to Reflect Great dreams, great plans, and great prayers have one thing in common—they focus on endeavors that require God's involvement and God's strength. Why settle for what is good when God offers you what is great? Why wish for the ordinary when God has provided means for you to experience the extraordinary? Begin today to trust his strength to accomplish the incredible in your family, in your school, in your students, and in yourself.

Talk to God just now about the areas where you feel weak, and ask him to be your source of strength. Thank him that there is literally no limit to that supply, for God's strength is as infinite as his love.

When God wants to move a mountain, he does not take a bar of iron, but he takes a little worm. The fact is, we have too much strength. We are not weak enough. It is not our strength that we want. One drop of God's strength is worth more than all the world.

—DWIGHT L. MOODY

To all who received him, who believed in his name, he gave power to become children of God.

John 1:12 NRSV

A Moment to Refresh

I know what it is to be in need, and I know what it is to have plenty. I have learned the secret of being content in any and every situation, whether well fed or hungry, whether living in plenty or in want. I can do everything through him who gives me strength.

Philippians 4:12–13

The Sovereign LORD gives me strength. He makes me sure-footed as a deer and keeps me safe on the mountains.

Habakkuk 3:19 GNT

The foolishness of God is wiser than man's wisdom, and the weakness of God is stronger than man's strength.

1 Corinthians 1:25

There is one source of power that is stronger than every disappointment, bitterness, or ingrained mistrust, and that power is Jesus Christ, who brought forgiveness and reconciliation to the world.

—JOHN PAUL II

We do not have a high priest who is unable to sympathize with our weaknesses, but we have one who has been tempted in every way, just as we are—yet was without sin. Let us then approach the throne of grace with confidence, so that we may receive mercy and find grace to help us in our time of need.

Hebrews 4:15–16

Since through God's mercy we have this ministry, we do not lose heart.... But we have this treasure in jars of clay to show that this all-surpassing power is from God and not from us.

2 Corinthians 4:1, 7

The Spirit helps us in our weakness. We do not know what we ought to pray for, but the Spirit himself intercedes for us with groans that words cannot express.

Romans 8:26

O Lord, I do not pray for tasks equal to my strength: I ask for strength equal to my tasks.

—PHILLIPS BROOKS

God Alone Satisfies

A Moment to Pause

Set aside some time just now to enjoy the satisfaction of spending a few moments with God. Review the events of your day as you relax. What encounters took place with students or others that were particularly satisfying? How does the satisfaction you experienced in these occurrences differ from the satisfaction you experience with the Lord?

The quest for satisfaction is a daily part of each person's life. Sometimes the quest is as simple as opening the refrigerator to find a dish to appease your hunger. Other times the quest is as complex as searching for a person to fulfill your need for relationship.

Yet the reality is that you cannot be truly satisfied by temporal provisions or persons. Not long after eating a feast, you hunger. Soon after taking a drink, you thirst. If blessed with a friend who fulfills one facet of your being, you find she lacks what you need for another facet. If blessed with wealth, you find some money merely brings the desire for more money.

This quest for satisfaction leads ultimately to God, for he offers satisfaction not of the flesh but of the soul, not temporal but eternal, not finite but infinite.

There is only one being who can satisfy the last
aching abyss of the human heart,
and that is the Lord Jesus Christ.
—Oswald Chambers

A Moment to Reflect Though you rightly offer thanks for temporal blessings, receive them as reminders that only God fully satisfies the deepest longings of your soul. In what areas does your soul hunger or thirst today? Have you put unrealistic pressure on the people or possessions in your life to fulfill those empty places? Look to God for satisfaction instead. Tell him openly of your need and let him guide you to the spring of his fulfillment.

By finding satisfaction in your relationship with the Lord, you become like a spring of water. You find refreshment for your own soul, and you have resources with which God refreshes those around you. For the Lord is your source, and he does not run dry.

The satisfaction of man can never come out of anything that is finite. Man can only be satisfied with the very fullness of God. There is no satisfaction in things sensuous, in things material, in things finite. If we want rest, contentment, completeness, and peace, we must find these in the infinite.
I adjure you to look to Christ.

—JOSEPH PARKER

*Satisfy us in the morning with your unfailing
love, that we may sing for joy and be glad all
our days.*

Psalm 90:14

A Moment to Refresh

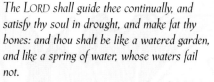

*The LORD shall guide thee continually, and
satisfy thy soul in drought, and make fat thy
bones: and thou shalt be like a watered garden,
and like a spring of water, whose waters fail
not.*

Isaiah 58:11 KJV

*Praise the LORD, O my soul; all my inmost
being, praise his holy name. Praise the LORD,
O my soul, and forget not all his benefits—who
forgives all your sins and heals all your
diseases, who redeems your life from the pit and
crowns you with love and compassion, who
satisfies your desires with good things so that
your youth is renewed like the eagle's.*

Psalm 103:1–5

*Jesus said, "Whoever drinks the water I give
him will never thirst. Indeed, the water I give
him will become in him a spring of water
welling up to eternal life."*

John 4:14

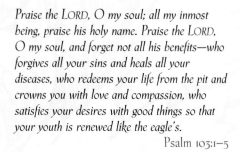

Thou shalt ever joy at eventide if thou spend the day fruitfully.

⤳

—*Thomas à Kempis*

Do not store up for yourselves treasures on earth, where moth and rust destroy, and where thieves break in and steal. But store up for yourselves treasures in heaven, where moth and rust do not destroy, and where thieves do not break in and steal. For where your treasure is, there your heart will be also.

Matthew 6:19–21

Oh that men would praise the LORD for his goodness, and for his wonderful works to the children of men! For he satisfieth the longing soul, and filleth the hungry soul with goodness.

Psalm 107:8–9 KJV

The Lord said: "I will refresh the weary and satisfy the faint."

Jeremiah 31:25

Let temporal things serve thy use, but the eternal be the object of thy desire.

⤳

—*Thomas à Kempis*

Trusting God

A Moment to Pause

Retreat to a place of quiet stillness. Settle into a favorite resting spot and be aware of God's presence there with you. Spend a few moments recalling specific times in your life when God has proven himself trustworthy. Let images of those instances flow through your mind as if pages of a photo album. Such images are reassuring to the heart, and trusting the purely spiritual is what God asks you to do.

Even in the most dire circumstances—when you perceive no trace of his presence in your life, when the evidence suggests you have been abandoned and indicators imply he has not been faithful, when you no longer have even the slightest emotion to encourage you in his way—God asks you to trust what you cannot see, what you cannot prove, and what you cannot feel. He asks you to trust the purely spiritual. He asks you to simply trust him.

Why is this type of trust so important in the Lord's eyes? Because when you stop believing only what you can see and start believing God for the things you can't, you are living by faith.

Quiet minds that rest in God cannot be perplexed or frightened, but go on in fortune or misfortune at their private pace, like a clock during a thunderstorm.
—Robert Louis Stevenson

A Moment to Reflect

When first you entered into relationship with God through Christ, you trusted him not only with your life, but with your eternity as well. Does it not seem odd, then, that you sometimes have difficulty trusting him with a particular circumstance now? This seeming discrepancy occurs because trust does not happen once for all. Trust is a conscious and continual choice that requires the submission of your personal reason, of your personal emotions, and of your personal will.

Make the conscious choice today to trust God with each of the particular circumstances that have worried your thoughts and consumed your emotions. Let him prove himself to you once more, adding yet another page to the photo images in your heart and mind.

Do not look forward to the changes and chances of this life in fear; rather look to them with full hope that, as they arise, God, whose you are, will deliver you out of them. He is your keeper. He has kept you hitherto. Do you but hold fast to his dear hand, and he will lead you safely through all things.

—Francis of Sales

73

May the God of hope fill you with all joy and peace as you trust in him, so that you may overflow with hope by the power of the Holy Spirit.

Romans 15:13

A Moment to Refresh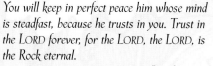

You will keep in perfect peace him whose mind is steadfast, because he trusts in you. Trust in the LORD forever, for the LORD, the LORD, is the Rock eternal.

Isaiah 26:3–4

Do not fret because of evil men or be envious of those who do wrong; for like the grass they will soon wither, like green plants they will soon die away. Trust in the LORD and do good; dwell in the land and enjoy safe pasture.

Psalm 37:1–3

Happy are those who have the God of Jacob to help them and who depend on the LORD their God, the Creator of heaven, earth, and sea, and all that is in them. He always keeps his promises.

Psalm 146:5–6 GNT

Put thou thy trust in God,
In duty's path go on;
Walk in His strength with faith and hope,
So shall thy work be done.

—PAUL GERHARDT, TRANSLATED BY JOHN WESLEY

The LORD is good, a refuge in times of
trouble. He cares for those who trust in him.
                                    Nahum 1:7

In God, whose word I praise, in the LORD
whose word I praise—in God I trust; I will
not be afraid. What can man do to me?
                                    Psalm 56:10–11

Blessed is the man who trusts in the LORD,
whose confidence is in him. He will be like a
tree planted by the water that sends out its
roots by the stream. It does not fear when
heat comes; its leaves are always green. It
has no worries in a year of drought and
never fails to bear fruit.
                                    Jeremiah 17:7–8

*All God's giants
have been weak
men, who did great
things for God
because they
believed that God
would be with
them.*

—HUDSON TAYLOR

Time to Refocus

A Moment to Pause

Come aside today and enjoy a few moments alone with the Lord. Share with him the details of your day. Thank him for that person who encouraged or helped you. Tell him about the problems you have encountered, that complaint that hurt you, that criticism that marred your day. Allow God to refresh your soul and refocus your outlook.

Have you ever closely examined the leaf of a tree? If so, you probably noticed some dirt on the leaf. You might have seen a little brown spot, a small tear, or even a ragged hole. For even on a healthy tree, a leaf is rarely perfect or spotless. Leaves have insects that attack them, strong winds that batter them, and a host of other natural elements that can harm them. If you focused on each individual leaf and removed the ones that were not perfect, you would soon have a leafless tree.

Yet God has a larger purpose for the tree than you can discover by focusing on individual leaves. He can take imperfect parts and create a thing of beauty. By taking a step away from the leaf and focusing on the tree as a whole, one can discover a wondrous work of God's design.

The Bible has a great deal to say about suffering
and most of it is encouraging.
—A. W. Tozer

A Moment to Reflect

It is easy to be nearsighted regarding the events of your day or the effectiveness of your work. Individual difficulties can crowd your thoughts, taint your emotions, and even paralyze you into inaction. During such times, pause and take a step back. Ask God to help you refocus your vision. Know he has a larger purpose than individual difficulties indicate. Trust him to create a wondrous work of his design in your life.

Just as the elements that challenge a tree make it stronger in the long run, Scripture promises many benefits when you trust God to work through the challenges in your life. As you meditate on the following verses, consider which benefits God is building into your life just now.

No words can express how much the world owes to sorrow. Most of the Psalms were born in a wilderness. Most of the Epistles were written in a prison. The greatest poets have "learned in suffering what they taught in song." Take comfort, afflicted Christian! When God is about to make pre-eminent use of a person, He puts them in the fire.

⁓

—GEORGE MACDONALD

*Blessed is the man who perseveres under trial,
because when he has stood the test, he will
receive the crown of life that God has promised
to those who love him.*

James 1:12

A Moment to Refresh

*I consider our present sufferings not worth
comparing with the glory that will be revealed in
us.... And we know that in all things God
works for the good of those who love him who
have been called according to his purpose.*

Romans 8:18, 28

*We never become discouraged.... Our spiritual
being is renewed day after day. And this small
and temporary trouble we suffer will bring us a
tremendous and eternal glory, much greater than
the trouble. For we fix our attention, not on
things that are seen, but on things that are
unseen. What can be seen lasts only for a time,
but what cannot be seen lasts forever.*

2 Corinthians 4:16–18 GNT

There has never yet been a man in our history who led a life of ease whose name is worth remembering.

༈

—THEODORE ROOSEVELT

Consider it pure joy, my brothers, whenever you face trials of many kinds, because you know that the testing of your faith develops perseverance. Perseverance must finish its work so that you may be mature and complete, not lacking anything.

James 1:2–4

Our mouths were filled with laughter, our tongues with songs of joy. Then it was said among the nations, "The LORD has done great things for them." The LORD has done great things for us, and we are filled with joy. Restore our fortunes, O LORD, like streams in the Negev. Those who sow in tears will reap with songs of joy. He who goes out weeping, carrying seed to sow, will return with songs of joy, carrying sheaves with him.

Psalm 126:2–6

God will never permit any troubles to come upon us unless he has a specific plan by which great blessing can come out of the difficulty.

༈

—PETER MARSHALL

Choose to Do Good

A Moment to Pause

Who has God used today to demonstrate his goodness to you? Likewise, how has he used you to demonstrate his goodness to another? Slip away to enjoy a few moments of quiet reflection, and turn your thoughts toward the Lord. Meditate on his goodness toward you.

Good deeds never happen without a conscious choice. That is why the simple statement in Acts 10:38, "Jesus went about doing good," makes such a dramatic impact on our hearts. Consistently making the conscious choice to do good is a dramatically different lifestyle, and that lifestyle makes a dramatic impact in the lives of the people it touches.

People sometimes concentrate solely on the conscious choice to refrain from evil. Yet that choice alone is not enough to fulfill all God wants to do in and through our lives, for that choice does not automatically result in actions that are good. By focusing merely on refraining from evil, we often end up doing nothing at all. Instead, God desires that we live in continual awareness of the needs around us and purposefully choose to respond to those needs.

We have a call to do good, as often as we have
the power and the occasion.
—William Penn

A Moment to Reflect

Are you sometimes afraid of doing good because of what it might cost you in time, finances, emotions, or other personal resources? Recognize today that you do not sacrifice yourself when you do good deeds; rather, you invest yourself. That is why the results of good deeds grow and multiply and can even produce dividends that are eternal.

Become passionate about doing good, and thereby live a life of purpose and significance. Even the smallest act of goodness can make a big difference in someone's life. Choose now to make a difference in someone's life each day. The happy outcome is that your life will be greatly blessed as well. You cannot serve God's goodness to another without receiving a taste of it yourself.

Make a rule, and pray to God to help you to keep it, never, if possible to lie down at night without being able to say, I have made one human being a least a little wiser, a little happier, or a little better this day.

—GEORGE MacDONALD

Love must be sincere. Hate what is evil; cling to what is good. Be devoted to one another in brotherly love. Honor one another above yourselves.

Romans 12:9–10

A Moment to Refresh

The fruit of the Spirit is love, joy, peace, patience, kindness, goodness, faithfulness, gentleness and self-control. Against such things there is no law.

Galatians 5:22–23

Do not forget to do good and to share with others, for with such sacrifices God is pleased.

Hebrews 13:16

Do not withhold good from those who deserve it, when it is in your power to act. Do not say to your neighbor, "Come back later; I'll give it tomorrow"—when you now have it with you.

Proverbs 3:27–28

Do what is right and good in the LORD's sight, so that it may go well with you.

Deuteronomy 6:18

Well done is better than well said.

⁓

—BENJAMIN FRANKLIN

Jesus said, "You are the light of the world. A city on a hill cannot be hidden. Neither do people light a lamp and put it under a bowl. Instead they put it on its stand, and it gives light to everyone in the house. In the same way, let your light so shine before men, that they may see your good deeds and praise your Father in heaven."

Matthew 5:14–16

It is by grace you have been saved, through faith—and this not from yourselves, it is the gift of God—not by works, so that no one can boast. For we are God's workmanship, created in Christ Jesus to do good works, which God prepared in advance for us to do.

Ephesians 2:8–10

Measure your day, not by what you harvest, but by what you plant.

⁓

—AUTHOR UNKNOWN

Giving Again

A Moment to Pause

Slow down, both physically and mentally, for a few minutes. Enjoy the simple pleasure found in sipping a cup of hot tea, basking in a ray of sunshine, or soaking in a tepid bath. Feel the warmth permeate your muscles, easing their tension and encouraging them to let go of the stresses of the day.

As you experience this physical warmth, think about a special moment that brought warmth to your heart recently. Envision the smiling face of a child in your class. Recall an expression of gratitude from a parent or coworker. Remember the last time you realized you had made a difference in the life of a student. These are the moments that bring meaning and fulfillment to the lives of teachers. These are the moments that say that something worthwhile has been given.

Why is it that nothing warms the hearts of teachers quite like the realization that what we have given has been welcomed and received? It is because real teachers give more than assignments. They give more than instruction and more than guidance. They even give more than knowledge.

Real teachers give a part of themselves, a part that comes from the heart.

We make a living by what we get.
We make a life by what we give.
—Duane Hulse

A Moment to Reflect

Because your gift to others is personal, it is often draining. Perhaps there are days when you feel you have given all you can, days when you fear you have nothing left to give. During times like these, you must learn to be a receiver. Just as an orchard tree must regularly receive warmth and nourishment in order to bear fruit, a teacher must regularly receive restoration and renewal in order to give again.

If you need to receive new strength right now, know that God is near. He is waiting to fill and restore you. Tell him about your needs. Then open your heart to receive all he is waiting to give.

Lord, each child seeks to find in me
a heart that cares and eyes that see,
till I am drained of energy.
I need Your touch.

Please fill me with Your peace again.
Restore my spirit from within.
Renew the heart of me, for then
I will give much.

ॐ

—*Melinda Mahand*

In everything I did, I showed you that by this
kind of hard work we must help the weak,
remembering the words the Lord Jesus himself
said: "It is more blessed to give than to
receive."

Acts 20:35

A Moment to Refresh

The LORD is my shepherd,
I shall not want.
He makes me lie down in green pastures;
He leads me beside quiet waters.
He restores my soul;
He guides me in the paths of righteousness
For His name's sake.

Psalm 23:1–3 NASB

Every good and perfect gift is from above,
coming down from the Father of the heavenly
lights, who does not change like shifting
shadows.

James 1:17

O God, you are my God, earnestly I seek you;
my soul thirsts for you, my body longs for you,
in a dry and weary land where there is no
water.... Because your love is better than life,
my lips will glorify you.... My soul will be
satisfied as with the richest of foods; with
singing lips my mouth will praise you.

Psalm 63:1, 3, 5

In this life it is not what we take up but what we give up that makes us rich.

જે

—HENRY WARD BEECHER

Remember this: Whoever sows sparingly will also reap sparingly, and whoever sows generously will also reap generously. Each man should give what he has decided in his heart to give, not reluctantly or under compulsion, for God loves a cheerful giver. And God is able to make all grace abound to you, so that in all things at all times, having all that you need, you will abound in every good work.

2 Corinthians 9:6–8

Happy are those who reject the advice of evil people, who do not follow the example of sinners or join those who have no use for God. Instead, they find joy in obeying the Law of the Lord, and they study it day and night. They are like trees that grow beside a stream, that bear fruit at the right time, and whose leaves do not dry up.
They succeed in everything they do.

Psalm 1:1–3 GNT

It is possible to give without loving, but it is impossible to love without giving.

જે

—RICHARD BRAUNSTEIN

Sh!

A Moment to Pause   Finding a moment of quietness can be a challenge when active students, hectic schedules, and over-commitments crowd your life. Nevertheless, seek to find a few precious moments of stillness. Listen to the quiet and experience the peace it affords your soul.

Now imagine taking a jar half-filled with soil and half-filled with water. When you shake the jar, turbulence mixes the soil and water, giving you a murky liquid of indistinct ingredients. When you set the jar aside for a while, however, the various elements settle into distinctly identifiable layers. Any particles of rock or sand settle on the bottom. Loamy clay soil settles atop the rock and sand, and bits of decaying leaves or twigs rise to the top.

In much the same way, the turbulence of life can easily scatter our thoughts and reduce our plans and priorities to disarray. Setting aside moments to be silent and still is crucial for the restoration of our souls. During these quiet times, the important elements of life come sharply back into focus. We are able to identify specific matters for prayer and for action. We are able to regain the perspective needed to reprioritize and reorganize as well.

A closed mouth gathers no foot.
—Author Unknown

A Moment to Reflect

Mother Teresa once said, "The beginning of prayer is silence," and so it should be. Silence provides time to still the mind. Silence teaches patience, and, above all, it teaches listening skills. If you wait quietly for the Lord, you hear when he speaks to your heart. You become ready to receive his Word as well.

Set aside a few moments today simply to rest quietly before the Lord. Ask him to refresh your spirit and speak to your heart during this time. Allow that stillness to be a quiet prelude to a time of heart-to-heart communion with God.

Be still, my soul! thy God doth undertake
To guide the future as He has the past.
Thy hope, thy confidence let nothing shake;
All now mysterious shall be bright at last.
Be still my soul! the waves and winds still know
His voice who ruled them while He dwelt below.

—KATHARINA VON SCHLEGEL

The LORD is good to those whose hope is in him, to the one who seeks him; it is good to wait quietly for the salvation of the LORD.

Lamentations 3:25–26

A Moment to Refresh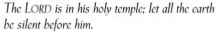

Be still, and know that I am God.

Psalm 46:10

The LORD is in his holy temple; let all the earth be silent before him.

Habakkuk 2:20

Be still before the LORD and wait patiently for him; do not fret when men succeed in their ways, when they carry out their wicked schemes.... A little while, and the wicked will be no more; though you look for them, they will not be found. But the meek will inherit the land and enjoy great peace.

Psalm 37:7, 10–11

For God alone my soul waits in silence

Psalm 62:1 NRSV

True silence is the rest of the mind. It is to the spirit what sleep is to the body—nourishment and rest.

—WILLIAM PENN

This is what the Sovereign Lord, the Holy One of Israel, says: "In repentance and rest is your salvation, in quietness and trust is your strength."

Isaiah 30:15

For God alone my soul waits in silence, for my hope is from him. He alone is my rock and my salvation, my fortress; I shall not be shaken.

Psalm 62:5–6 NRSV

The fruit of righteousness will be peace; the effect of righteousness will be quietness and confidence forever.

Isaiah 32:17

Better a dry crust with peace and quiet than a house full of feasting, with strife.

Proverbs 17:1

Be silent, and God will speak again.

—FRANÇOIS DE SALIGNAC DE LA MOTHE FÉNELON

Seeing God's Blessings

A Moment to Pause

As you come aside for quiet reflection, imagine yourself on the seashore, your bare toes touching the white-frothed ripples of water that lap the shore. What do you see there? From a standing perspective, you might see a passing ocean liner on the horizon. By kneeling down and looking from a closer perspective, you might notice tiny froth bubbles popping on the sand. If you wade out farther and put your face beneath the surface, your underwater perspective might reveal a school of small silvery fish. In short, what you see depends completely on your position and your perspective. So consider today: have you seen any of God's blessings recently?

Each day your spiritual position influences how you view all that happens around you. For instance, if you recognize you are positioned in God's hands, that his will orders your life and protects your endeavors, then you expect to see evidence of his working. You recognize his hand of blessing when it appears.

In addition, your perspective influences your view. Sometimes you may miss God's blessings because you are looking far off into the future. Yet God's blessings are always near at hand. Watch from a closer perspective.

Reflect upon your present blessings—of which
every man has many—not on your past
misfortunes, of which all men have some.
—Charles Dickens

A Moment to Reflect The person who looks for God's hand in life is the one who recognizes God's blessing. For example, two people can look at the same fruit tree in spring. While one says, "The tree has no fruit," the other says, "The tree is bursting with buds." The person who recognized God's hand at work was the person who was blessed.

Start now by acknowledging God's common blessings of sunshine and water, food and shelter. Consider what life would be like if he withdrew even one of these blessings. Anything you enjoy beyond these common blessings is a personal blessing from the Lord. Begin today to watch expectantly for his hand on your life. Then thank him for the abundant blessings that result.

Be the eye of God dwelling with you
The foot of Christ in guidance with you
The shower of the Spirit pouring on you
Richly and generously.

⌇

—ALEXANDER CARMICHAEL

May God be gracious to us and bless us and make his face shine upon us... that your ways may be known on earth, your salvation among all nations.

Psalm 67:1–2

A Moment to Refresh

Praise be to the God and Father of our Lord Jesus Christ, who has blessed us in the heavenly realms with every spiritual blessing in Christ.

Ephesians 1:3

A faithful man will be richly blessed.

Proverbs 28:20

The LORD bless you and keep you; the LORD make his face shine upon you and be gracious to you.

Numbers 6:24–25

*I will always thank the LORD;
I will never stop praising him....
Find out for yourself how good the Lord is.
Happy are those who find safety with him.*

Psalm 34:1, 8 GNT

*The whole world is ordered and arranged to match
and meet the needs of the people of God.*

～

—J. A. MOTYER

Blessed are they whose ways are blameless,
who walk according to the law of the Lord.
Blessed are they who keep his statutes and
seek him with all their heart.

Psalm 119:1–2

The blessing of the LORD brings wealth,
and he adds no trouble to it.

Proverbs 10:22

Blessed are those you choose and bring
near to live in your courts! We are filled
with the good things of your house, of your
holy temple.

Psalm 65:4

You will eat the fruit of your labor;
blessings and prosperity will be yours.

Psalm 128:2

*The Christian tastes
God in all his
pleasures.*

～

—J. I PACKER

Seek and Find

A Moment to Pause

Have you noticed how everything in nature must look outside itself to find its needs met? The flower thirsts for moisture and so awaits the rainfall. The honeybee possesses no sweet substance within itself but must go to the blossom to gather nectar. The wheat requires sunlight before being fit for harvest. Similarly, we do not possess the resources to meet our inner needs. We must go outside ourselves to fulfill soul-needs such as love, acceptance, and belonging, for such needs can be met only within the context of a relationship. Today, God waits to see where we will go.

Some people seek a relationship with another person to meet needs. Others attempt a relationship with the physical satisfaction of pastimes like eating or exercising. Still others seek a relationship with material possessions. Eventually, however, you will discover that no other person, no amount of physical satisfaction, and no amassing of material gain can truly fulfill the gaping chasm of need within your soul. You can end up hurting yourself and others because you sought fulfillment in the wrong places.

God's good news is that he has provided for every thirst of your soul. Today he waits, hoping and longing for us to seek him.

He waits to be wanted.
—*A. W. Tozer*

A Moment to Reflect

When God calls you to seek him, do not imagine he is suggesting that you participate in hide-and-seek as if you were a child playing games. The riches of a relationship with the Lord are already provided for you. He simply wants you to want him, to choose to pursue him with all your heart rather than to pursue the empty pleasures of this world.

Just as a close relationship with another person requires time and intent, an intimate relationship with the Lord requires time and intent as well. Seek him today through his Word and through prayer. He promises to be found. Soon you will know him as the living God, present with you, living in you, and supplying you with all that you need.

You called, you cried, you shattered my deafness,
you sparkled, you blazed, you drove away my
blindness, you shed your fragrance, and I drew
in my breath, and I pant for you.

ॐ

—AUGUSTINE OF HIPPO

Let us try to know the LORD. He will come to
us as surely as the day dawns, as surely as the
spring rains fall upon the earth.

Hosea 6:3 GNT

A Moment to Refresh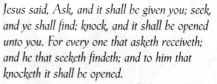

Jesus said, Ask, and it shall be given you; seek,
and ye shall find; knock, and it shall be opened
unto you. For every one that asketh receiveth;
and he that seeketh findeth; and to him that
knocketh it shall be opened.

Luke 11:9–10 KJV

You will find God if you look for him with all
your heart and with all your soul.

Deuteronomy 4:29

The LORD is good unto them that wait for him,
to the soul that seeketh him.

Lamentations 3:25 KJV

May all who seek you rejoice
and be glad in you.

Psalm 40:16

At any moment and in any circumstance, the soul that seeks God may find Him, and practice the presence of God.

ॐ

—BROTHER LAWRENCE

When you search for me, you will find me; if you seek me with all your heart. I will let you find me, says the LORD.

Jeremiah 29:13–14 NRSV

Those who know your name will trust in you, for you, LORD, have never forsaken those who seek you.

Psalm 9:10

May all who seek you rejoice and be glad in you.

Psalm 70:4

Let the hearts of those who seek the LORD rejoice. Look to the LORD and his strength; seek his face always.

1 Chronicles 16:10–11

God is great, and therefore He will be sought;

God is good, and therefore He will be found.

ॐ

—AUTHOR UNKNOWN

There Is a Comforter

A Moment to Pause

Is there a place in your soul that yearns for comfort today? You cannot long interact with this world without receiving a criticism that discourages, a rejection that paralyzes, or some heartfelt wound that dampens your desires and consumes your energy. Yet who can truly speak to your need when you are sick at heart? Listen closely, for there is one who can comfort you and, in that comfort, give you the strength and the hope to carry on.

The Lord offers you today a comfort that is more than mere emotional pacification. What lasting benefit is there in a comfort that simply soothes, caresses, embraces, or quiets? Though such sentimental comfort is sweet for the moment, its effect, like a tranquilizing drug, wears away, and you are left once again disabled by your throbbing pain.

The comfort of God, however, is poured down upon you from all that is majestic, mighty, and immeasurable in him. Divine comfort is the very encouragement of God, the loving touch of the Most High applied to the human heart and mind. His comfort revives your energy, restores your spirit, and brings forth the power and hope to serve him once again.

*In times of affliction we commonly meet with
the sweetest experiences of the love of God.*
—John Bunyan

A Moment to Reflect

Although the comfort of good friends is often welcome, God alone knows precisely which part of your heart is wounded. He understands that a piece of your spirit has been robbed. You are comforted when God recovers that piece which you had lost to despair. You are comforted when he brings you that lost piece and says, *I restore you to wholeness. Be well.*

Ask God to look into your heart just now. Feel free to talk to him about your feelings and your needs. Whatever is the cause of your pain, be assured his purposes of right will stand upon the ruins of all wrong. His comfort will cause you to rise again in triumph, strengthened and restored once more.

He giveth more grace
when the burdens grow greater,
He sendeth more strength
when the labors increase;
To added affliction he addeth his mercy,
To multiplied trials, his multiplied peace.

—ANNIE JOHNSON FLINT

Whenever I am anxious and worried, you comfort me and make me glad.

Psalm 94:19 GNT

A Moment to Refresh

Praise be to the God and Father of our Lord Jesus Christ, the Father of compassion and the God of all comfort, who comforts us in all our troubles, so that we can comfort those in any trouble with the comfort we ourselves have received from God.

2 Corinthians 1:3–4

Blessed are they that mourn: for they shall be comforted.

Matthew 5:4 KJV

Why are you cast down, O my soul, and why are you disquieted within me? Hope in God; for I shall again praise him, my help and my God.

Psalm 42:5–6 NRSV

We can sometimes see more through a tear than through a telescope.

ॐ

—AUTHOR UNKNOWN

Jesus said, I will pray the Father, and he shall give you another Comforter, that he may abide with you for ever.

John 14:16 KJV

Remember your word to your servant, in which you have made me hope. This is my comfort in my distress, that your promise gives me life.

Psalm 119:49–50 NRSV

"Comfort my people," says our God. "Comfort them!"

Isaiah 40:1 GNT

Jesus said, I will not leave you comfortless: I will come to you.

John 14:18 KJV

I pray that God may answer, in His own way, to your soul, and that He may be to you the God of all consolations.

ॐ

—SAMUEL RUTHERFORD

The Power of Trusting

A Moment to Pause

Have you ever been in a relationship where someone you trusted proved untrustworthy? Such experiences leave you in a weak and vulnerable position where you can easily be hurt. Because of that experience, you might have trouble associating a trust with anything other than vulnerability. God invites you to enter a different type of trust—a trust that places you in a position not of weakness, but of power.

In some ways your relationship with God is similar to that of a bear cub ambling by its mother's side. The cub has no need to rely on its own strength, for it has behind it the full power of the parent. What might have been a threat to the cub alone poses no threat at all when the mother is present.

Likewise, when you trust in God, you have access to the full range of his power. What might have been a threat or challenge to you is no longer, for God is all-powerful. His infinite power is placed at your disposal. In fact, Scripture states that all things become possible for those who trust him.

He who trusts in God can do all things.
—Alphonsus Liguori

A Moment to Reflect

What challenging task or conflict do you face this week? Do not feel pressured to focus on your power alone, trying to assess whether you are personally equal to the challenge. Instead, consider whether the Lord is equal to the challenge. Turn to him in trust and draw strength from the infinite source of the almighty God.

God's power, of course, does not ensure that you will never again face a struggle, that words or actions of others will never again hurt you. God's power does ensure that the Lord has a purpose for any struggle he brings you through—and he *will* bring you through. Trust him and be strong.

'Tis so sweet to trust in Jesus,
Just to take Him at His word,
Just to rest upon His promise,
Just to know "Thus sayeth the Lord."

I'm so glad I've learned to trust Him,
Precious Jesus, Savior, Friend;
And I know that He is with me,
Will be with me to the end.

—LOUISA M. R. STEAD

All things are possible to him that believeth.

Mark 9:23 KJV

A Moment to Refresh

Commit your way to the LORD; trust in him,
and he will act.

Psalm 37:5 NSRV

Jesus said, "Do not let your hearts be troubled.
Believe in God, believe also in me.... Very truly,
I tell you, the one who believes in me will also
do the works that I do and, in fact, will do
greater works than these, because I am going to
the Father. I will do whatever you ask in my
name, so that the Father may be glorified in the
Son. If in my name you ask me for anything, I
will do it."

John 14:1, 12–14 NRSV

Whoever goes to the LORD for safety, whoever
remains under the protection of the Almighty,
can say to him, "You are my defender and
protector. You are my God; in you I trust."

Psalm 91:1–2 GNT

Trusting means drawing on the inexhaustible resources of God.

~

—AUTHOR UNKNOWN

God is my savior; I will trust him and not be afraid. The LORD gives me power and strength; he is my savior.

Isaiah 12:2 GNT

He who gives attention to the word shall find good, and blessed is he who trusts in the LORD.

Proverbs 16:20 NASB

We have put our hope in the living God, who is the Savior of all men, and especially of those who believe.

1 Timothy 4:10

The LORD's unfailing love surrounds the man who trusts in him. Rejoice in the LORD and be glad, you righteous; sing, all you who are upright in heart!

Psalm 32:10–11

Trust is not the attitude that keeps you out of the storm; it is the attitude that carries you safely through.

~

—MELINDA MAHAND

A Wonder Worker

A Moment to Pause Perhaps today you feel your time has been filled with nothing but the rather ordinary—routine papers to fill out, mundane tasks to complete, customary conversations, and unremarkable encounters. If so, come away just now and refresh your soul as you reflect on the wondrous nature of God. Spend a few moments considering his incredible work in creation as well as in your personal life.

People today are more accustomed to marveling at Hollywood's special effects than to marveling at the canopy of a starry sky or at the blowing of the wind. In fact, one can easily go through days completely oblivious to the truly marvelous.

Part of the reason for this apathy may be the great strides of science during this lifetime. You and your peers have watched as new forms of energy, new plant and animal life, new stars, and even new galaxies have been discovered.

Yet you must remind yourself that these wonders are not truly new. Only your discovery of them is. All that has been done is to find creations that already existed and assign names to them. Such discoveries should cause you to marvel all the more at the Wonder-worker who is your God.

God moves in a mysterious way
His wonders to perform.
—William Cowper

A Moment to Reflect

Consider today that a god who could be measured and understood would be no god at all. Your God, however, cannot be completely fathomed or anticipated. There is no other like him. There is no standard by which to measure his works, no formula by which to understand. Therefore, you wonder and worship.

Have you recently neglected to marvel because you have not trusted God for marvelous things in your life? Recall the promise of Scripture that God can do more than you can ask as well as more than you can imagine. In fact, the Bible says you cannot even measure how much more he can do than you imagine. He is indeed a wonder worker.

How wondrous the Hand who once painted the sky,
Who set winds in motion and taught birds to fly.
Yet greater a wonder than all I can see
Is the new creature He fashioned in me.

How wondrous the Love who once came here to die,
Who lifted His own Son against a dark sky.
Yet greater a wonder than sin's costly toll
Is the assurance He lives in my soul.

—MELINDA MAHAND

109

*Who is like you, O LORD, among the gods?
Who is like you, majestic in holiness, awesome
in splendor, doing wonders?*

Exodus 15:11 NRSV

A Moment to Refresh

*You answer us by giving us victory, and you do
wonderful things to save us. People all over the
world and across the distant seas trust in you....
The whole world stands in awe of the great
things that you have done. Your deeds bring
shouts of joy from one end of the earth to the
other.*

Psalm 65:5, 8 GNT

*Give thanks unto the LORD, call upon his name,
make known his deeds among the people. Sing
unto him, sing psalms unto him, talk ye of all
his wondrous works.*

1 Chronicles 16:8–9 KJV

*I will praise you, O LORD, with all my heart; I
will tell of all your wonders.*

Psalm 9:1

Whenever God is at work there is the inexplicable.

⸎

—RALPH P. MARTIN

To him who is able to do immeasurably
more than all we ask or imagine, according
to his power that is at work within us, to
him be glory in the church and in Christ
Jesus throughout all generations, for ever
and ever!

Ephesians 3:20–21

LORD, you are my God; I will honor you
and praise your name. You have done
amazing things.

Isaiah 25:1 GNT

He is the living God and he endures
forever; his kingdom will not be destroyed,
his dominion will never end. He rescues
and he saves; he performs signs and
wonders in the heavens and on the earth.

Daniel 6:26–27

*God can do more in
a moment than man
in a millennium.*

⸎

—JOHN BLANCHARD

Remember Mercy

A Moment to Pause

Times of personal struggle are often seared into our minds even though we would rather forget them. Perhaps today such memories can begin to become blessings in your life as well as in the lives of those around you. Spend time alone today recalling your embarrassment and pain the last time you messed up at work or at home, had difficulty learning a new concept or skill, or struggled with strong emotion or temptation. Then consider whether anyone showed you mercy. If so, what effect did mercy have? If not, how do you think mercy might have helped?

Mercy is the result of one person understanding another person's struggle and behaving toward the person with compassion and understanding. The Bible explains that God has mercy on us because he understands what it is like to be human. (See Psalm 103:13–14 and Hebrews 2:17, 4:15.)

Likewise we extend mercy to those around us when we remember what their particular struggles are like. Mercy is not simply feeling sorry for someone or having a gush of emotion. Mercy is an action and as such is a conscious choice. We do not act mercifully because we feel like it. We act mercifully because we choose to.

Mercy is compassion in action.
—Author Unknown

Mercy exhibits itself in everyday situations. Mercy helps correct an accidental mess or mistake without fussing. Mercy helps a person learn a new concept or skill without becoming frustrated. Mercy remembers the strong pull of emotion or temptation, and looks upon a person's wrong choice with compassion and understanding rather than raw anger.

In order to meet the opportunity to exhibit mercy as a teacher, stay in touch with what it is like to be a student. Choose to learn something new this week. Then watch for opportunities to show mercy as you go through your day. When you behave toward someone else with mercy, you become a visible example of the very mercy of God.

There's a wideness in God's mercy,
Like the wideness of the sea.
There's a kindness in His justice,
Which is more than liberty.

For the love of God is broader
Than the measures of man's mind;
And the heart of the Eternal
Is most wonderfully kind.

—FREDERICK WILLIAM FABER

Thou art a gracious God, and merciful, slow to anger, and of great kindness.

Jonah 4:2 KJV

A Moment to Refresh

God says, "I will have mercy on whom I have mercy, and I will have compassion on whom I have compassion." It does not, therefore, depend on man's desire or effort, but on God's mercy.

Romans 9:15–16

He has showed you, O man, what is good. And what does the Lord require of you? To act justly and to love mercy and to walk humbly with your God.

Micah 6:8

Praise be to the God and Father of our Lord Jesus Christ! In his great mercy he has given us new birth into a living hope through the resurrection of Jesus Christ from the dead, and into an inheritance that can never perish, spoil or fade—kept in heaven for you.

1 Peter 1:3–4

Mercy, also, is a good thing, for it makes men perfect, in that it imitates the perfect Father. Nothing graces the Christian soul as much as mercy.

—AMBROSE

You have heard of Job's patience, and you know how the Lord provided for him in the end. For the Lord is full of mercy and compassion.

James 5:11 GNT

He that followeth after righteousness and mercy findeth life, righteousness, and honour.

Proverbs 21:21 KJV

Our God is merciful and tender. He will cause the bright dawn of salvation to rise on us.

Luke 1:78 GNT

Praise the LORD of hosts: for the LORD is good; for his mercy endureth for ever.

Jeremiah 33:11 KJV

Mercy imitates God and disappoints Satan.

—JOHN CHRYSOSTOM

Life-Changing Victory

Today you can change your life with one simple change of perspective. Begin to view life's challenges and struggles from the perspective of heaven rather than from the perspective of this world. Sound difficult? Really, it's not.

Consider the struggle of a hatching chick as it works to be freed from its shell. From the chick's perspective, the struggle is a mighty life–or–death battle. To us, the battle seems inconsequential. After all, the chick has only to defeat a fragile eggshell! Even when considering the chick's size and strength in proportion to the eggshell, we must remember God designed chicks for this very battle. He has already planned and provided for the chick to have victory and stand triumphantly on the other side, strengthened and better prepared for the future because of the struggle.

Likewise, your battles seem like life–or–death struggles to you. They require all the energy, strength, and persistence you have. To God, they are no more a threat than a fragile eggshell. In fact, Scripture declares that God has already planned and provided for you to have victory, knowing you will be strengthened and better prepared for the future because of the struggle.

You can fight with confidence where you are
sure of victory. With Christ and for Christ
victory is certain.
—Bernard of Clairvaux

A Moment to Reflect

Are you in a battle today? Consider that God has already provided for your victory and claim your triumph in Christ.

Remember, too, that your greatest victories do not take place outside, but rather they take place within the innermost part of your being. You cannot achieve spiritual strength by living a life free of conflict and trial. Only through struggle does the soul learn to rely on prayer; only through struggles does the mind learn to focus on the eternal; only through struggle does the will learn not to be ruled by emotion. Truly, there is no greater victory than the victory of your own soul.

A mighty fortress is our God,
A bulwark never failing;
Our helper He amid the flood
Of mortal ills prevailing.

And tho this world, with devils filled,
Should threaten to undo us,
We will not fear, for God hath willed
His truth to triumph thru us.

⌣

—MARTIN LUTHER

117

Thanks be to God, who always leads us in triumph in Christ, and manifests through us the sweet aroma of the knowledge of Him in every place.

2 Corinthian 2:14 NASB

A Moment to Refresh

Jesus said, "In the world you have tribulation, but take courage; I have overcome the world."

John 16:33 NASB

May those who love God be like the sun when it rises in its strength.

Judges 5:31

Thanks be to God! He gives us the victory through our Lord Jesus Christ.

1 Corinthians 15:57

Greater is he that is in you, than he that is in the world.

1 John 4:4 KJV

The LORD is my strength and my song, and is become my salvation.

Psalm 118:14 KJV

A victory inside us is ten thousand times more glorious than any victory can be outside of us.

∿

—HENRY WARD BEECHER

Yours, O LORD, are the greatness, the power, the glory, the victory, and the majesty; for all that is in the heavens and on the earth is yours; yours is the kingdom, O LORD, and you are exalted as head above all. Riches and honor come from you, and you rule over all. In your hand are power and might; and it is in your hand to make great and to give strength to all.

1 Chronicles 29:11–12 NRSV

O sing to the LORD a new song, for He has done wonderful things, His right hand and His holy arm have gained the victory for Him.

Psalm 98:1 NASB

Everyone born of God overcomes the world. This is the victory that has overcome the world, even our faith.

1 John 5:4

A victorious Christian life is not a superior brand of Christianity reserved for the elite of the elect. It is the normal Christian life for every Christian.

∿

—RONALD DUNN

Choosing Faith

A Moment to Pause

How many people in your life today have exhibited faith? Actually, all of them have. Everyone believes and makes decisions every day based on the objects of faith. Sometimes one puts in emotions and allow feelings to dictate behavior. Sometimes one places faith in other people and make choices based on their attitudes and opinions. And sometimes one places faith in outward circumstances that control the ever-changing events of the moment.

Yet biblical faith calls you to a radically different choice. When God asks you to have faith, he realizes the object of your faith makes all the difference. You might believe your six-year-old can drive your car to the store. Regardless of how strongly you believe that proposition, your belief does not make it so. A licensed driver would be the only reliable person for that task.

Similarly, God knows he is the only unchanging, fully reliable object for your faith. God asks you to make the conscious choice to believe his Word instead of believing what circumstances tell you, what emotions tell you, or what other people tell you. This is biblical faith.

Walking by faith means being prepared to trust where we are not permitted to see.
—*John Blanchard*

A Moment to Reflect

Perhaps you have been reluctant to live by faith, thinking it an apathetic acceptance of whatever may occur in life. Perhaps you have been discouraged, thinking faith is a type of sixth sense you must somehow possess. Such misconceptions can easily deter you from a life of faith.

Recognize today that biblical faith is active and practical. It is a burning power, a tremendous energy, infused into you by the object of your faith, the Word of God. Faith strengthens your spirit and builds in you the self-control not to reel from emotions, faint from circumstance or be persuaded by rumor, but rather to stand solidly upon God's Word because your God cannot lie.

I prayed for faith and thought it would strike me like a bolt of lightning, but faith did not come. One day I read, "Now faith comes by hearing and hearing by the word of God." I had closed my Bible and prayed for faith. I now began to study my Bible and faith has been growing ever since.

༄

—*D. L. MOODY*

In the gospel a righteousness from God is revealed, a righteousness that is by faith from first to last, just as it is written: "The righteous will live by faith."

Romans 1:17

A Moment to Refresh

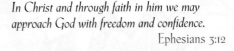

In Christ and through faith in him we may approach God with freedom and confidence.

Ephesians 3:12

Now that we have been put right with God through faith, we have peace with God through our Lord Jesus Christ. He has brought us by faith into this experience of God's grace, in which we now live. And so we boast of the hope we have of sharing God's glory!

Romans 5:1–2 GNT

We live by faith, not by sight.

2 Corinthians 5:7

Sovereign Lord, I put my hope in you; I have trusted in you since I was young. I have relied on you all of my life.

Psalm 71:5–6 GNT

Faith is the grip which connects us with the moving energy of God.

∿

—AUGUSTUS H. STRONG

Faith is being sure of what we hope for and certain of what we do not see.

Hebrews 11:1

If you have faith as a mustard seed, you can say to this mountain, "Move from here to here" and it will move. Nothing will be impossible for you.

Matthew 17:20

Faith comes from hearing the message, and the message is heard through the word of Christ.

Romans 10:17

May the God of hope fill you with all joy and peace as you trust in him, so that you may overflow with hope by the power of the Holy Spirit.

Romans 15:13

Let us step out into the darkness and reach out for the hand of God. The path of faith and darkness is so much safer than the one we would choose by sight.

∿

—GEORGE MACDONALD

A Waiting Friend

A Moment to Pause Today you have probably spent much time listening. Students, family members, coworkers—they come to you with their questions, comments, concerns, and needs. Yet where can you turn when you need to reveal the concerns of your heart? To whom can you describe your feelings and voice your hopes? Right this moment there is someone waiting to listen and longing to help. You already know him as Father and Lord. Now get to know him even better. Get to know him as Friend.

Consider the amount of time usually required for two people to become the kind of good friends who share openly and honestly with one another. Such relationships take months, if not years, to develop. Still sometimes we feel there are certain aspects of ourselves that we cannot share even with the best of friends.

When you turn to the Lord as your Friend, however, you are instantly in a relationship where you are known completely and loved intimately. He knows all about your past, your dreams, your struggles, and your fears. You have nothing to hide. He is ready to listen and is both willing and able to offer you comfort, guidance, strength—whatever your need just now.

Prayer is not wrestling with God's reluctance to bless us; it is laying hold of his willingness to do so.
—John Blanchard

A Moment to Reflect

Does your friendship with God seem a little lopsided? He knows all about you, but do you feel you do not know him as well? He loves you completely, but are you still learning to love? Do not let those feelings make you feel guilty or keep you from turning to God as a friend. You grow in your relationship with God in the same way you grow in your relationship with anyone. You spend time with him. You talk to him. You listen to him.

Begin to spend time each day talking to God. Listen for him to answer you in prayer or through the message of his Word. He is waiting to be your Friend.

How can I comprehend a God who waits for me,
Who longs to show compassion ever endlessly?
And how can I respond to grace that reaches
through eternity,
Except to wait, to long, to reach for You?

So though I hurry through the busy tasks of day,
Though all the moments of the evening slip away,
Still I will listen in my heart to hear
You when You softly say,
"Come, for I wait, I long, I reach for you."

—MELINDA MAHAND

God has surely listened and heard my voice in prayer. Praise be to God, who has not rejected my prayer or withheld his love from me!

Psalm 66:19–20

A Moment to Refresh

Therefore the LORD longs to be gracious to you, and therefore He waits on high to have compassion on you. For the Lord is a God of justice; How blessed are all those who long for Him. O people in Zion, inhabitant in Jerusalem, you will weep no longer. He will surely be gracious to you at the sound of your cry; when He hears it, He will answer you.

Isaiah 30:18–19 NASB

Give ear to my words, O LORD, consider my sighing. Listen to my cry for help, my King and my God, for to you I pray.

Psalm 5:1–2

O LORD, be gracious to us; we long for you. Be our strength every morning, our salvation in time of distress.

Isaiah 33:2

To know how to speak to God is more important than knowing how to speak to men.

—ANDREW MURRAY

The prayer of a righteous man is powerful and effective.

James 5:16

I sought the LORD, and he answered me; he delivered me from all my fears. Those who look to him are radiant; their faces are never covered with shame.

Psalm 34:4–5

"Before they call, I will answer; while they are still speaking I will hear," says the LORD.

Isaiah 65:24

I called on your name, O LORD, from the depths of the pit. You heard my plea: "Do not close your ears to my cry for relief." You came near when I called you, and you said, "Do not fear."

Lamentations 3:55–57

The goal of prayer is the ear of God.

—C. H. SPURGEON